This book belongs to

Words and Thoughts to Help You Grow

Words and Thoughts to Help You Grow

Kenneth N. Taylor

Illustrated by Kathryn E. Shoemaker

INSPIRATIONAL PRESS

NEW YORK

Previously published in three separate volumes:

BIG THOUGHTS FOR LITTLE PEOPLE, copyright © 1983 by Kenneth N. Taylor; artwork, copyright © 1983 by Kathryn E. Shoemaker.
GIANT STEPS FOR LITTLE PEOPLE, copyright © 1985 by Kenneth N. Taylor and Mark D. Taylor; artwork, copyright © 1985 by Kathryn E. Shoemaker.
WISE WORDS FOR LITTLE PEOPLE, copyright © 1987 by Kenneth N. Taylor; artwork, copyright © 1987 by Kathryn E. Shoemaker.

All Scripture verses from this book are from *The Living Bible,* © 1971 by Tyndale House Publishers.

First Inspirational Press edition published in 1998.

Inspirational Press
A division of BBS Publishing Corporation
386 Park Avenue South
New York, NY 10016

Inspirational Press is a registered trademark of BBS Publishing Corporation.

Published by arrangement with Tyndale House Publishers, Inc.

Library of Congress Catalog Card Number: 98-72395

ISBN: 0-88486-220-8

Printed in Hong Kong.

Contents

BIG THOUGHTS
for little people

A WORD TO PARENTS (and Grandparents)

Many years ago my little book *The Bible in Pictures for Little Eyes* was quietly introduced to Christian parents in America, and now there are a million copies in print in thirty languages around the world. My purpose was to help little children learn about the Bible and God.

This book, *Big Thoughts for Little People*, has a different purpose. Its value is in teaching small children about Christian living—that is, how to be good! This is one of the great themes of the Bible, and it is very important for little children to be taught right from wrong (as well as simple courtesy and good manners).

A word about the wonderful artwork is in order. There are surprises in every picture. For instance, how many ladybugs can you and your child find on the cover? (I see six of them!) There are ladybugs hiding in each illustration. You'll also have fun finding all the objects on each page which begin with the theme letter.

The questions are a very important part of each lesson. Questions that are thought-provoking but not hard to answer are of great importance in the learning process.

And please don't skip the Bible verses. Children will learn them easily, and they will stay in the mind and heart for life.

KENNETH N. TAYLOR

A is for Asking.
We ask when we pray.
God's happy to answer
And help us each day.

The boy and his father are praying. Can you see them?
It is bedtime, and they are talking to God. They are asking
God to take care of them and they are saying, "Thank
you" for all the kind things God does for them. God wants us
to talk with him. He wants to be our friend. We can pray
anytime, wherever we are, because God always hears us.

SOME QUESTIONS TO ANSWER
1. What are the boy and his father doing?
2. Point to the bears who are thankful to God for their food.
3. What are some things you are thankful for? Let's pray
   now and tell God, "Thank you."

A BIBLE VERSE FOR YOU TO LEARN
Tell God your needs and don't forget to thank him for his answers.

PHILIPPIANS 4:6

B's for Behave;
It means doing what's right.
Be happy and helpful;
Don't argue or fight.

Do you know what "behave" means? It means doing what your parents ask you to do. It also means playing nicely with other children. In this picture some of the children and animals are behaving and some are not. Look at the girls fighting over an ice cream cone. I think the ice cream cone is going to fall to the ground. Then neither of the girls will have it. But the puppies know better. They are sharing.

SOME QUESTIONS TO ANSWER
1. Are the little girls behaving? What are they doing?
2. Point to the puppies. Are they behaving?
3. What are the children at the table doing?

A BIBLE VERSE FOR YOU TO LEARN
Jesus said, "If you love me, obey me." JOHN 14:15

C is for Crying.
It hurts when you fall,
But please do not cry
About nothing at all.

Can you see what happened to the little girls on the tricycles? They bumped into each other, and one girl has fallen off. Ouch! That hurts. Perhaps she bumped her head. I think she's going to cry. What would you do if you fell off? Would you cry? It's all right to cry if you're hurt. Crying will help you feel better. But if you're not really hurt, try to smile. Smiling will also help you feel better.

SOME QUESTIONS TO ANSWER
1. Why is the girl crying?
2. Is it all right to cry if you're hurt?
3. Should you cry every time you get a little bump?

A BIBLE VERSE FOR YOU TO LEARN
A cheerful heart does good like medicine. PROVERBS 17:22

D is for Doing
What needs to be done.
So please do it cheerfully;
Then you'll have fun.

All these children are doing nice things to help each other. One boy is helping the teacher wash the dishes. He must be careful not to drop and break them. One of the girls is helping by watering the flowers. One of the boys is pulling a girl and her bear in the wagon. We should treat others just as we want them to treat us. God is happy when we do helpful and kind things for one another.

SOME QUESTIONS TO ANSWER
1. What is the duck doing?
2. How are the children doing kind things for one another? Tell about each one.
3. What kind thing could you do to help someone?

A BIBLE VERSE FOR YOU TO LEARN
Do for others what you want them to do for you. MATTHEW 7:12

E is for Everyone.
God loves us all:
The black and the white,
And the short and the tall.

Everyone in the world is special to God. We are all different, but he loves all of us. There are many colors of hair and many colors of skin. Some children are tall, some are short. Some are fat, some are thin. In this country we live in houses or apartments. In some countries, the children live in houses made of straw or bamboo. Do you see all of the different children playing together in the picture? God loves all of them.

SOME QUESTIONS TO ANSWER
1. What color is your hair?
2. Find the boy driving the train. What color is his hair?
3. Does God love all the children? Does God love you?

A BIBLE VERSE FOR YOU TO LEARN
See how very much our heavenly Father loves us, for he allows us

to be called his children. 1 JOHN 3:1

's for Forgive
If a girl or a boy
Is naughty or careless
And breaks your new toy.

Do you see what the bear has done? He has broken the toy frog. If someone did that to you, you might be angry. Perhaps you would want to get even with him by doing something bad to him. But that isn't the way God wants you to act. He wants you to forgive. He does not want you to hurt people who do something wrong to you. He wants you to be good to them. That isn't easy, but God will help you.

SOME QUESTIONS TO ANSWER
1. Look at the children playing in the sandbox. What are they doing?
2. Should those children continue fighting, or should they forgive each other?
3. Did someone hurt you or hurt your feelings today? Did you forgive him?

A BIBLE VERSE FOR YOU TO LEARN
Be kind to each other, tenderhearted, forgiving one another. EPHESIANS

4:32

G is for God;
He's your Father above.
He made you and likes you
And shows you his love.

God lives in heaven, far up above the sky, but he is also here with us. Can you see God in the picture? No, we can't see him, but he can see us. He loves us and always wants to help us. He made the earth and sky and flowers and everything there is. But even though he is so great and strong, he thinks about us all the time. He wants us to think about him and love him too.

SOME QUESTIONS TO ANSWER
1. Who made the flowers? Who made you?
2. Where is God? Can you see him? Can he see you?
3. Does God love you? Do you love him?

A BIBLE VERSE FOR YOU TO LEARN
The Lord God made the earth and the heavens. GENESIS 2:4

H is for Helping
Your mother or dad.
It says in the Bible
That this makes God glad.

God tells us in the Bible to be kind to others and to help them.
Sometimes that isn't easy, because we want to do things to
please ourselves instead of helping others. Look at all the
children in the picture who are helping. Some are helping
collect eggs. Others are helping with the small animals.
God wants us to be cheerful helpers. That means not to
complain when you are asked to help. God will help you be a
cheerful helper if you ask him to.

SOME QUESTIONS TO ANSWER
1. Point to all the children who are helping. What is each
   one doing?
2. Were you a helper today? What did you do?
3. What can you do tomorrow to be a helper? Ask your
   mother or father to remind you to be a helper.

A BIBLE VERSE FOR YOU TO LEARN
God will bless you and use you to help others. 1 TIMOTHY 4:16

is for Illness,
It keeps you in bed.
But soon you'll feel fine
And be playing instead.

It isn't fun to be sick, but it happens to all of us once in awhile. Usually you feel better soon, but sometimes you need to go to the doctor to get medicine or a shot. You might even have to go to the hospital. Some children live in countries where there aren't very many doctors to help. In those countries the children are sick more often and sometimes it takes much longer for them to get well. Isn't it wonderful to live where there are doctors to help us? We should thank God for doctors when we pray.

SOME QUESTIONS TO ANSWER
1. Have you ever been sick?
2. Did you go to the doctor?
3. What did the doctor do?

A BIBLE VERSE FOR YOU TO LEARN
I was sick and you visited me. MATTHEW 25:36

J is for Joyful;
It means full of cheer.
Have fun and be happy
Each day of the year.

Christmas is a joyful time. It is the celebration of Jesus' birthday. It reminds us about God and how much he loves us. We decorate Christmas trees and give presents to each other. We like to sing Christmas carols. We can also be joyful every day of the year. We can thank God for our families. We can play with our friends. We can help other people. These things all make us joyful.

SOME QUESTIONS TO ANSWER
1. What kind of tree is in the picture?
2. Are the children in the picture being joyful or sad?
3. What are some things that make you joyful?

A BIBLE VERSE FOR YOU TO LEARN
Always be full of joy in the Lord. PHILIPPIANS 4:4

K is for Kindness
To Grandpa and Gram;
Be helpful to others,
Be sweet as a lamb!

These children are visiting their grandparents and are being kind to them. Being kind means being friendly to people and helping them. Some people are mean and not kind at all. They want everything for themselves. They don't stop to think about what other people want. When they act that way, they are being unkind. But God wants us to help others and to be friendly to them. He wants us to be kind.

SOME QUESTIONS TO ANSWER
1. Have you ever been mean and unkind? Tell about it.
2. Tell about something you did to be kind to someone.
3. Does God want you to be kind or unkind?

A BIBLE VERSE FOR YOU TO LEARN
You should practice tenderhearted mercy and kindness to others.

COLOSSIANS 3:12

L is for Lying,
A thing not to do.
No matter what happens,
Don't say what's not true.

Look at the broken window. The boy's baseball went through the window. Have you ever broken something and then said you didn't do it? That would be lying instead of telling the truth, and God doesn't like lies. I hope the boy tells the truth about the broken window. Why do people tell lies? I think it is because they don't want to be scolded or punished for what they have done. But God wants us to tell the truth, even if it means we will be punished.

SOME QUESTIONS TO ANSWER
1. What happened to the window?
2. Does God want us to tell lies?
3. Can you think of a time when you wanted to tell a lie, but told the truth instead?

A BIBLE VERSE FOR YOU TO LEARN
You must not lie. EXODUS 20:16

LEMONADE
5¢

M is for Messy,
With toys on the floor;
So pick them up neatly
When playtime is o'er.

Some boys and girls leave their toys on the floor where people can fall over them and get hurt and break the toys. Wouldn't it be better to pick up the toys and put them away when you are through playing with them? Usually this makes everyone happier. It is also good to make your bed look neat in the morning and after a nap. And you can clear the table after meals and help wash and dry the dishes so they won't be messy.

SOME QUESTIONS TO ANSWER
1. What is the girl doing to her bed?
2. What should the children do with the toys on the floor?
3. Do you pick up your toys when you are finished playing with them?

A BIBLE VERSE FOR YOU TO LEARN
God is not one who likes things to be disorderly and upset. 1 CORIN

THIANS 14:33

N is for Nice;
It is always worthwhile.
Be pleasant to others
And give them a smile.

Do your parents ever tell you to be nice? What do they mean?
Perhaps you have been playing too roughly or have hit
someone or been quarreling. When they tell you to be nice
they mean you should stop doing those things. They want you
to be pleasant and helpful. When you are nice, everyone
is happy. When you do something naughty, everyone is sad.

SOME QUESTIONS TO ANSWER
1. Did you do anything today that wasn't nice? What was it?
2. Did you do something nice today? What was it?
3. What can you do tomorrow to be nice?

A BIBLE VERSE FOR YOU TO LEARN
Happy are the kind and merciful.   MATTHEW 5:7

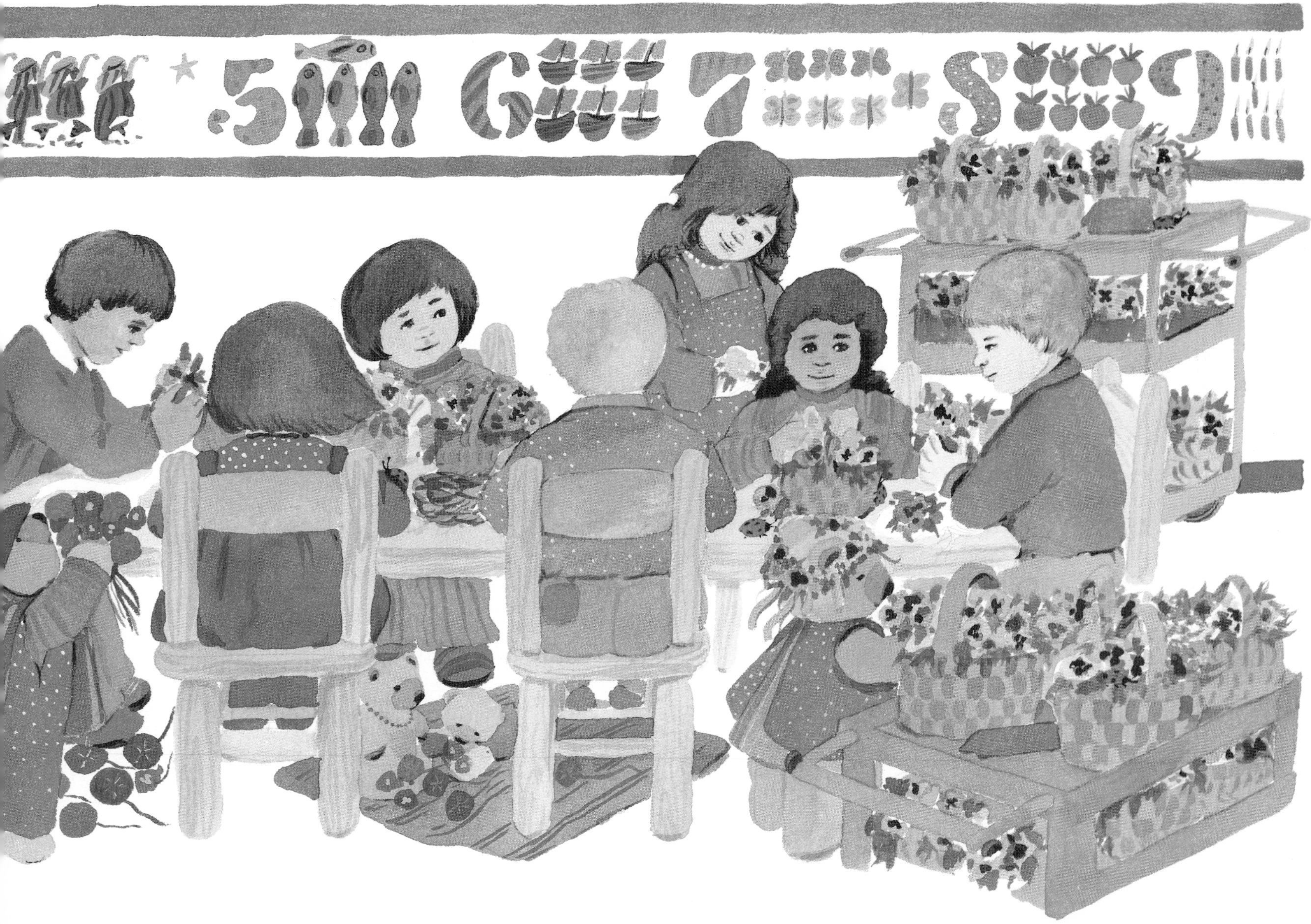
5 6 7 8 9

O's for Obey.
When you do as you're told,
It makes parents glad;
They won't spank you or scold.

God tells us to obey our parents. He says this is very important because our parents know what is best for us. We will be happiest if we obey our parents. God says that fathers and mothers should punish their children when they don't obey. If you are punished, it will help you remember to obey your parents. And after they have punished you, your parents will give you a big hug and will tell you how much they love you. Then everyone will be happy.

SOME QUESTIONS TO ANSWER
1. Where do you think the little girl is going?
2. What does God say your parents should do if you don't obey?
3. Who is happy when you obey?

A BIBLE VERSE FOR YOU TO LEARN
Children, obey your parents. This is the right thing to do. EPHESIANS

6:1

P's for Polite,
Saying, "Thank you" and "Please."
It's easy to do
And puts others at ease.

When you ask for something, it is more polite to say, "May I please have it?" than to say, "Gimme that!" And when someone gives you something, it is polite to say, "Thank you." Being polite shows respect. That means you think the other person is as good as you are, or even better. God wants us to respect other people, so he likes it when we are polite. He doesn't want us to think we are better than others.

SOME QUESTIONS TO ANSWER
1. Point to the children in the picture who are being polite.
2. Tell some ways you can be polite.
3. Does God want us to be polite? Why?

A BIBLE VERSE FOR YOU TO LEARN
Honor your father and mother. EPHESIANS 6:2

is for Quarrel;
Each wants the first turn.
But waiting for others
Is not hard to learn.

Oh, dear me! Look at those children quarreling. Each one is mad at everyone else! Is this good? No! Everyone is being selfish and wants things for himself instead of sharing with the others. Is there a way to solve their problem? I hope someone shows them how to play nicely together. You can learn to share and be kind to your playmates. Then they will learn to share too. You can be the one to show them how to share.

SOME QUESTIONS TO ANSWER
1. Why are the children in the picture quarreling?
2. Do you ever quarrel? About what?
3. How can you stop a quarrel?

A BIBLE VERSE FOR YOU TO LEARN
Quarreling, harsh words, and dislike of others should have no place

in your lives. EPHESIANS 4:31

R is for Resting,
Like taking a nap,
Or sometimes just sitting
On mother's soft lap.

Sometimes we all need to stop working or playing to take a rest. That is the way God made us. He wants us to be rested because then we are happier. If you don't get enough rest you will probably be cross and unhappy. Then everyone else will be unhappy too. Nap time is a good time. You can lie in bed and think pleasant thoughts, and all of a sudden you'll be asleep. Then when you wake up you'll be happy as a songbird. Maybe you will sing!

SOME QUESTIONS TO ANSWER
1. How many children in the picture are resting?
2. Why do you feel better after your nap?
3. What can happen when you get too tired?

A BIBLE VERSE FOR YOU TO LEARN

God wants his loved ones to get their proper rest. PSALM 127:2

S is for Singing;
We sing when we're glad.
It might even help you
To sing when you're sad.

Everyone likes to sing. There are happy songs and sad songs, funny songs and serious songs. We can sing while we play or while we take a walk. Some people like to sing in the bathtub or in the shower. God likes to hear us sing. He made us with voices that can sing. Singing makes us happy, and God wants us to be happy. Singing can even help us feel happy when we are sad. I hope you know lots of songs.

SOME QUESTIONS TO ANSWER
1. Which child is dressed up like a ladybug?
2. Do you like to sing?
3. What are some songs you know?

A BIBLE VERSE FOR YOU TO LEARN
Sing to the Lord with thankful hearts. COLOSSIANS 3:16

T is for Thankful;
Thank God for your lunch,
And thank him for dinner
And breakfast and brunch.

The children in the picture are thanking God for their food.
Many children in the world don't have enough to eat.
They are hungry all the time. But we have good breakfasts
and lunches and suppers, and sometimes even snacks in
between. So we should thank God every day that we have
enough to eat. That's why we bow our heads before we
eat and say, "Thank you" to God.

SOME QUESTIONS TO ANSWER
1. What are some things you are thankful for?
2. Who are some people you are thankful for?
3. When should we thank God for food?

A BIBLE VERSE FOR YOU TO LEARN
Thank the Lord for all the glorious things he does. PSALM 105:1

FRIENDS EVERYWHERE

U's for Unselfish;
Be willing to share.
Be thoughtful of others
And always be fair.

A selfish person wants the first turn, the biggest cookie, and the best of everything. But an unselfish person is willing to let others go first or have the biggest cookie. When you share with your friends, you have more fun together. Sometimes it is very difficult, but God wants us to be unselfish, so that is the best thing to do. It is better to please God than to please ourselves. One good thing about sharing is that an unselfish person is happier than a selfish person.

SOME QUESTIONS TO ANSWER
1. Who is riding a unicycle?
2. Does God want us to be selfish or unselfish?
3. Can you think of some ways you can be unselfish?

A BIBLE VERSE FOR YOU TO LEARN
Don't think only of yourself. Try to think of the other person, too,

and what is best for him. 1 CORINTHIANS 10:24

V is for Visitors;
Help them have fun,
And play and be friendly
With all, not just one.

It is wonderful to have friends. You can go to their house to visit, or they can come to visit you. Sometimes you can eat lunch together, or you can play outside or have fun making things. When you have visitors you must remember to play happily together and take turns with your toys. And remember to play with each of your visitors, not just the ones you like best. Then everyone will have fun.

SOME QUESTIONS TO ANSWER
1. How many children in the picture are coming to visit?
2. Tell the names of your friends who come to your house to visit.
3. What are some things you do together?

A BIBLE VERSE FOR YOU TO LEARN
Cheerfully share your home with those who need a meal or a place

to stay for the night. 1 PETER 4:9

W's for Worship—
That's giving God praise
And telling our love for him
All of our days.

When you think about how great and good God is, and how much you love him, then you are worshiping him. You can thank God and worship him at church, or at home, or when you are all alone. Yes, you can talk to God wherever you are. You can think about how wonderful he is because he made the trees and grass and stars and sun and moon. And you can tell him, "Thank you" for making you and loving you.

SOME QUESTIONS TO ANSWER
1. In the picture, which things did God make?
2. Who loves you even more than your parents do?
3. Tonight when you go to bed you can worship God by thanking him for loving you and for making the sun and stars.

A BIBLE VERSE FOR YOU TO LEARN
All the earth shall worship you and sing of your glories. PSALM 66:4

X is for Xylophone—
Use it to play
Happy songs about Jesus
Throughout each new day.

Look at all the musical instruments in this picture. Can you find the xylophones? Have you ever played a xylophone? It makes pretty music, but it sounds very different from a piano or a violin. Do you think God likes to hear children play a xylophone? I think he does. God likes music. He especially likes it when we play or sing songs about him. He wants us to tell him how much we love him.

SOME QUESTIONS TO ANSWER
1. Have you ever played a xylophone?
2. What other instruments are the children playing?
3. Does God like to hear children making music?

A BIBLE VERSE FOR YOU TO LEARN
Make a joyful symphony before the Lord, the King. PSALM 98:6

Y is for Yelling—
It's all right outdoors;
But please be more quiet
In houses and stores.

Do you like to yell? I think most children do. Sometimes making a lot of noise is all right, but sometimes it isn't. Here are some times you should be quiet:

When your mother is resting or is tired.
When the baby is asleep.
When your parents have guests.
When you should be taking a nap.

SOME QUESTIONS TO ANSWER
1. Who is taking a nap in the hammock?
2. Who is sleeping in the tree?
3. When should you be quiet?

A BIBLE VERSE FOR YOU TO LEARN
If you shout a pleasant greeting to a friend too early in the morning,

he will count it as a curse! PROVERBS 27:14

Z is for Zebra
Or Zebu or Zoo.
God made all the creatures,
And he made you, too.

Do you know what a zoo is? It is a place where there are many, many kinds of animals and birds and snakes. There are even lions and tigers and bears. Have you ever been to a zoo? If so, you know how many kinds of animals there are. See if you can find some of them in the picture. Did you know that God made all these animals? God made the grass and trees and rocks and animals, and he made you a very special person.

SOME QUESTIONS TO ANSWER
1. Where are the zebras in the picture?
2. Which animals can the children pet?
3. Who made all the animals?

A BIBLE VERSE FOR YOU TO LEARN
The Lord said, "By my great power I have made the earth and all

mankind and every animal.” JEREMIAH 27:5

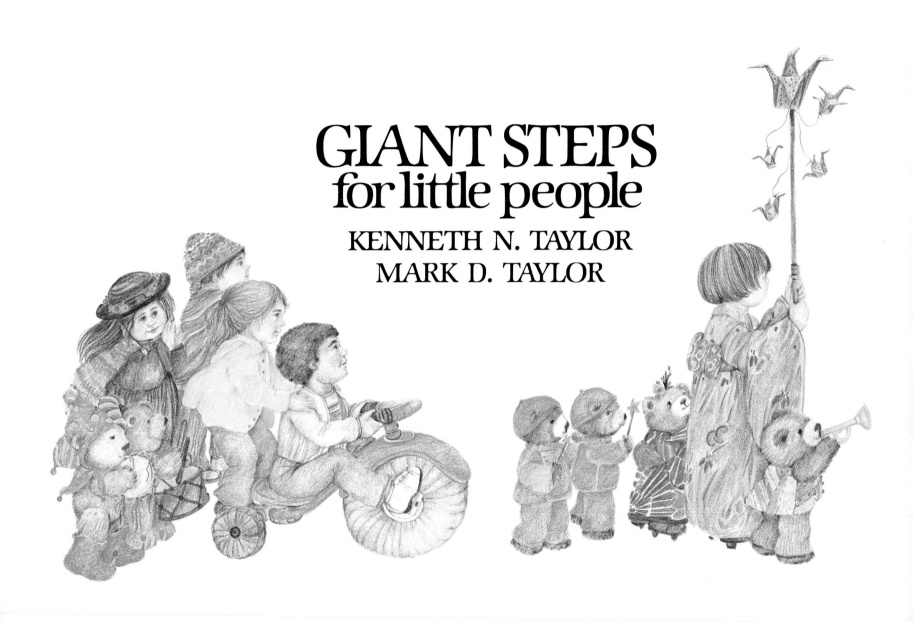

GIANT STEPS
for little people

KENNETH N. TAYLOR
MARK D. TAYLOR

A WORD TO PARENTS (and Grandparents)

Little eyes and ears are powerful. What they see and hear at an early age can deeply affect their entire lives. "Give me a child until he is five years old," it has been said, "and I will have directed his life forever." This statement is true. How important it is, then, to fill little minds with life-changing thoughts.

And what can be more important for a child's life than to know God's laws of right and wrong, and the instructions of Jesus about how to please God as told to us in the Sermon on the Mount?

These great truths are here broken into tasty, bite-sized morsels that a very young child can grasp and grow on. Kathryn Shoemaker's wonderful full-color pictures illustrate and enforce these deep truths.

Each page has a little prayer and a Bible verse. Young children can memorize quite easily, so I encourage you to help your child learn these verses. Picture books are soon outgrown, but Bible verses memorized in childhood last for a lifetime.

Pray with me that God will use this book to help your child, grandchild, or young friend "grow in the grace of our Lord Jesus Christ."

KENNETH N. TAYLOR

P.S. Don't forget to look for the ladybugs in every picture!

Love your father and your mother
And your brother, sister too.
But most of all and best of all,
Love God, for he loves you.

These children love their father and mother. God wants families to love each other. But I will tell you a secret. This family loves God even more than they love each other! And that's exactly what God wants. There are many reasons we should love God and thank him. Most of all, we love him because he loves us. You can thank him for giving you your wonderful parents. You can thank him for giving you enough good food to eat every day, and time to play, and friends. You should thank him for all these good things, and love him all the time.

SOME QUESTIONS TO ANSWER

1. Do these children love their father and mother? How can you tell?
2. Whom should we love more than anyone else?
3. What are some things you can thank God for?

A LITTLE PRAYER

Dear God, help me to love you very much all the time.

A BIBLE VERSE FOR YOU TO LEARN

Love the Lord your God with all your heart, soul, and mind. MATTHEW

22:37

Jesus said to love your neighbors.
Help them if you can,
Both now and as you grow to be
A lady or a man.

These people are Christmas caroling. It must be cold, because the children are wearing hats and scarves. Is the weather cold and snowy at Christmas where you live? It looks like the children are singing for their neighbors. This is wonderful, for Jesus said we should love our neighbors as much as we love ourselves. Can you name the people who live near you? They are your neighbors, and you should love them. Jesus wants you to love everyone you know. This is important to remember every day.

SOME QUESTIONS TO ANSWER
1. When we help each other, does this make God glad?
2. Can you name someone who is your neighbor?
3. How can you help him or her?

A LITTLE PRAYER
Dear Lord, help me to love everyone I know.

A BIBLE VERSE FOR YOU TO LEARN
Love your neighbor as much as you love yourself. MATTHEW 22:39

Some kids think they're very smart,
And then start feeling proud.
But all we have has come from God,
So don't be proud and loud.

The girl in the lookout tower thinks she is bigger and better than anyone else. She doesn't know something very important, and I'll tell you what it is. God doesn't like us to be proud and think we are better than other people. He wants us to realize he has made us just the way we are. If you can do something well, thank God for it. Don't act like a big shot. Each of us is better in some things and not as good in others. Each of us should thank God and not be proud.

SOME QUESTIONS TO ANSWER

1. Does God want you to be proud and think you are better than other people?
2. What are you good at doing? (Swimming? Picking up toys?)
3. Who made you better in doing some things and not as good in others?

A LITTLE PRAYER

Dear Father in heaven, thank you for making me good at _____ .

A BIBLE VERSE FOR YOU TO LEARN

Humble men are very fortunate, for the Kingdom of Heaven is given to

them. MATTHEW 5:3

Are you sad and lonely?
Do you want a better way?
Ask God to make you happy;
He can do it right away.

I see a little girl who is very sad. She is thinking about something that has happened that makes her sad. I wonder what it is. But she can be happy again. God can make her happy if she asks him to. He can make her realize how many nice things have happened to her. And she can be glad because God loves her. The next time you see someone who is sad, be God's little helper and go and cheer him up. Then three people will be happy —you, the person you have helped, and God will be happy too.

SOME QUESTIONS TO ANSWER

1. What do you think the girl is sad about?
2. Have you been sad today? What happened?
3. Teli about something you can do that helps you feel better when you are sad.

A LITTLE PRAYER

Dear God, thank you that you want to comfort me when I am sad.

A BIBLE VERSE FOR YOU TO LEARN
Those who mourn are fortunate, for they shall be comforted. MATTHEW

5:4

Gentleness is always good
Along with your rough play.
So even if you're big and strong
Be thoughtful every day.

Look at all the animals in the pet shop. How many of them can you name? I see rabbits and puppies, fish and chicks. I wonder if the giant birds are real or if they are toys! The children are treating the animals very gently. God wants us to be gentle with people, too. We shouldn't push them around or act like bullies. Instead, we should always try to help one another. Sometimes this is hard to remember, especially if someone pushes you first. But you can ask God to help you respond kindly, even if someone is mean to you.

SOME QUESTIONS TO ANSWER

1. What animals do you see in the picture? Can you see any ladybugs?
2. Are you bigger and stronger than someone else you know? Who is it?
3. Should you get what you want by taking it away from someone who isn't as strong as you are?

A LITTLE PRAYER

Dear God, my Father in heaven, please help me to be kind and gentle to others.

A BIBLE VERSE FOR YOU TO LEARN

The meek and lowly are fortunate, for the whole wide world belongs

to them. MATTHEW 5:5

If you do what's right and just
Because you really care,
Then God will smile,
  because he wants
To see you do what's fair.

Can you find all the children and bears who are hiding? The girl
standing behind the tree is counting while the others hide. Is
she watching the others while she counts? I hope not. That's
not the way to play the game. If she is watching where the others
hide, she is cheating. Did you know God can see you all the
time—even when you are playing? He is in heaven, but he is
also right here in this room. He is happy when you are doing
good things, but he is unhappy when you are unfair. I hope
you always try to make him happy by doing what is right.

SOME QUESTIONS TO ANSWER
1. Is God here in the room with us?
2. How can you make God happy?
3. What did you do today to make him happy?
   Did you do anything to make him sad?

A LITTLE PRAYER
Dear Father in heaven, please help me always to be fair.

A BIBLE VERSE FOR YOU TO LEARN
Happy are those who long to be just and good, for they shall be com

pletely satisfied. MATTHEW 5:6

Acting kind to others
After they've been bad to you
Means you are showing mercy,
And God is happy, too.

Oh my! Look at the huge mess. The girls were having a tea party, but now everything is on the floor. It looks like the boy's truck bumped into the table. I can tell the boy is sorry about the accident, and two of the girls are comforting him. They are saying, "It's all right. It was an accident. We'll help you pick everything up." I'm glad they didn't get angry with him. They are being merciful. You can be merciful by forgiving someone who has hurt you instead of trying to get even. God wants you to be merciful.

SOME QUESTIONS TO ANSWER
1. Point to the girls in the picture who are being kind and merciful.
2. What does it mean to be merciful?
3. Have you ever been merciful? Tell about a time when you helped someone who had been bad to you.

A LITTLE PRAYER
Dear God, help me to be kind to others, even when they have not been kind to me.

A BIBLE VERSE FOR YOU TO LEARN
Happy are the kind and merciful, for they shall be shown mercy.

MATTHEW 5:7

Programs on TV are sometimes good,
But often bad.
Don't watch or read of evil things,
For that will make God sad.

Look at the children watching TV. The little bear is hiding his eyes. He knows it isn't good to watch people who are being bad. If we watch them, we might decide to copy them and be bad too. Sometimes it seems like fun to be naughty, but God doesn't want us to do wrong things. He wants us to do what's right and kind and good. It is easier to do what's right when we think about good things. I'm glad most of the children are playing games or reading good books instead of watching the bad people on TV.

SOME QUESTIONS TO ANSWER
1. Why isn't the bear looking at the television?
2. Do you ever see anyone being bad on TV?
3. What do you think you should do when this happens?

A LITTLE PRAYER
Father in heaven, please help me always to do what's right and kind and good.

A BIBLE VERSE FOR YOU TO LEARN
Happy are those whose hearts are pure, for they shall see God.

MATTHEW 5:8

Don't get into arguments,
Just turn and walk away.
And try to help your friends
   have peace
In both their work and play.

What's going on here? There seems to be a war. The bears have been quarreling with one another, and now they are going to fight. What do you think the boy is telling the bears? I believe he's trying to get them to stop fighting. He wants them to be peaceful. God wants us to be peaceful, too. He doesn't want us to fight with our brothers or sisters or friends. And he wants us to keep others from fighting. He wants us to be peacemakers. He wants all of us to work and play happily together.

SOME QUESTIONS TO ANSWER
1. What are the bears in the picture doing?
2. What is the boy doing?
3. Does God want us to fight or to be peacemakers?

A LITTLE PRAYER
Please, dear God, help me not to quarrel. Help other people not to quarrel either.

A BIBLE VERSE FOR YOU TO LEARN
Happy are those who strive for peace—they shall be called the sons of

God. MATTHEW 5:9

Sometimes you'll be laughed at
When you try to do what's right;
But God is watching all you do
And he approves the sight.

I see someone doing something very naughty. The children are dumping over all the trash cans. Now the garbage is all over the street and the children have made the garbage collector's job very hard. They think it is fun to be bad. They told the girl to help them, but she won't do it. They laughed at her for being good. But the girl and the bears don't care. They want to please God instead of pleasing the other children. God is glad that the girl is obeying him and doing what is good.

SOME QUESTIONS TO ANSWER

1. What are the children doing?
2. Do you think God can see this big mess?
3. Are the girl and the bears going to be naughty too?

A LITTLE PRAYER

Dear God, help me always to do what is right, even if other people laugh at me.

A BIBLE VERSE FOR YOU TO LEARN

Happy are those who are persecuted because they are good, for the

Kingdom of Heaven is theirs. MATTHEW 5:10

If you say that you love God,
Some kids may laugh and jeer.
But don't let it upset you;
Just remember God is near.

Can you see all the people walking to church? But look! Four of the children are walking in the other direction. They are making fun of the people who are going to church and are telling them not to go. Perhaps they don't know that God would like them to go to church too. I'm glad no one is obeying those children. Sometimes it is very hard to do the right thing if others laugh at us. But we should ask God to help us do what is right. He will help us, even if others are making fun of us.

SOME QUESTIONS TO ANSWER

1. Where are most of the children going?
2. What are the other children doing?
3. Which children are making God glad?

A LITTLE PRAYER

Dear God, help me always to do right, even when others want me to do wrong.

A BIBLE VERSE FOR YOU TO LEARN

When you are laughed at because you are my followers—wonderful!

MATTHEW 5:11

Always try to do what's right,
And never do what's wrong.
Then others who are
     watching you
Will sing a happy song.

These children are helping in the garden. They all seem happy, and no one is being naughty or mean. They are doing what is right because they love God and want to please him. The neighbors are watching the children. I believe the neighbors will want to love God when they see how kind the children are to one another. But if children who love God are naughty or mean to one another, others will not want to love God. Often people pay more attention to what we do than what we say.

SOME QUESTIONS TO ANSWER

1. If you are unfriendly or naughty, will your friends want to become God's children?
2. Do you think the neighbors in the picture will want to love God?
3. How can you help other children want to love God?

A LITTLE PRAYER

Dear God, I want to be a good example to others in all I do.

A BIBLE VERSE FOR YOU TO LEARN

Let your good deeds glow for all to see, so that they will praise your

heavenly Father. MATTHEW 5:16

God wants you to share with others
All he's given you.
So give your money cheerfully,
And share your playthings too.

These children are bringing toys and boxes and cans of food to church! Are they going to have a picnic? No, the food is for families who do not have enough money to buy all the food they need. We can show we love God by giving food and toys to people who can't buy their own. We can also give some of our money to God by giving it to our church. Then some of the money will be used to send teachers to tell people about God and his love. Jesus said we should not love our money. We should use some of it to help others.

SOME QUESTIONS TO ANSWER
1. What are the children doing?
2. What will happen to the food?
3. Does God want us to use some of our money to help other people?

A LITTLE PRAYER
Our Father in heaven, thank you that we can help people who don't have enough food.

A BIBLE VERSE FOR YOU TO LEARN
Store treasures in heaven where they will never lose their value, and

are safe from thieves. MATTHEW 6:20

Worry means to think about Bad things that might come true. But God wants you to trust him; He will show you what to do.

It would be nice if no one ever got sick or hurt. But sometimes a child has a temperature or breaks an arm or leg. Does God know about it when you are sick or hurt? Yes! He is always looking down from heaven in love. Sometimes he keeps you from getting hurt, but sometimes he lets you get hurt! Either way he loves you just as much. If he lets you get hurt, does that mean he doesn't love you? Of course not! He loves you all the time, and he will be with you and help you all the time, even when you are sick or hurt.

SOME QUESTIONS TO ANSWER

1. What is happening in the picture?
2. Does God love you even when he lets you get sick or hurt?
3. Should you thank him for loving you all the time? Let's do it now.

A LITTLE PRAYER

Dear God, thank you for loving me and being with me all the time, even when I am sick or hurt.

A BIBLE VERSE FOR YOU TO LEARN

Don't be anxious about tomorrow. God will take care of your tomor

row too. Live one day at a time. MATTHEW 6:34

God can hear you praying,
Whether morning, noon, or night.
He answers, "Yes,"
    or answers, "No."
He knows what's best and right.

What is this family doing? That's right, they are praying. Perhaps
the children are thanking God for their mother and father,
and for their friends, and for a fun day. They may be thanking
God, or they may be asking him for something they want.
Sometimes God gives us exactly what we ask for, but sometimes
he says, "It wouldn't be good for you to have what you are
asking for!" Then God will say, "No" or "Not yet." We can trust
God to give us what is good and not give us what is bad for
us, even if we want it and ask him for it.

SOME QUESTIONS TO ANSWER
1. What do you think the children are talking to God about?
2. Does God always give us what we ask him for? What if we
   ask for something that is not good for us?
3. What are you thankful for?

A LITTLE PRAYER
Father in heaven, thank you that you always know what is best
for me.

A BIBLE VERSE FOR YOU TO LEARN
Ask and it will be given to you. MATTHEW 7:7

How should you treat others?
I will tell you what to do.
Be kind and also helpful,
Just as you want done to you.

These children are having a happy time on the merry-go-round. But I see something I don't like. A big boy is grabbing a balloon away from a little boy. Is that a good way for him to act? Of course not! How do you think the big boy would like it if somebody did that to him? He wouldn't like it at all. God tells us not to do anything to others we wouldn't want them to do to us. We should be as kind to others as we want them to be to us. That's the way God wants us to act.

SOME QUESTIONS TO ANSWER

1. Look at the picture and point to some children who are being kind. What are they doing?
2. Which boy is doing something naughty? What is he doing?
3. Do you want people to be nice to you? How should you treat them?

A LITTLE PRAYER

Dear Lord, help me to treat others just as I want them to treat me.

A BIBLE VERSE FOR YOU TO LEARN

Do for others what you want them to do for you. MATTHEW 7:12

Once I built a castle;
I was pleased as I could be.
But then the waves got bigger,
And they washed it out to sea.

Have you ever been to the beach and played in the sand? Maybe
you built a castle with wet sand, and then a big wave came
and knocked it down! That's what is happening in the picture.
The children have spent a long time building their castle,
but now it is all going to fall down. Too bad! But look at the
children who are building a castle on the rocks. The water
will not knock it down. Those children are wise. Jesus says you
are wise, too, if you do whatever God tells you to do. You
are like the wise children who are building their castle on the
rocks.

SOME QUESTIONS TO ANSWER
1. What happens when waves hit a sand castle?
2. Are the children wise to build a castle on the rocks? Why?
3. Are you wise when you do whatever God wants you to do?

A LITTLE PRAYER
Dear God in heaven, I want to be wise and do what you want
me to do.

A BIBLE VERSE FOR YOU TO LEARN
All who listen to my instructions and follow them are wise, like a man

who builds his house on solid rock. MATTHEW 7:24

The Bible is the Word of God,
Its stories all are true.
If you can't read,
   I'm sure your mom
Or dad will read to you.

Can you see what is happening in the picture? The children's father is reading a book to them. It's a very special book filled with stories from the Bible. The Bible has many wonderful true stories about people who lived many years ago. It tells us about God and about God's love for us. And the Bible tells us how God wants us to live. The Bible is the most important book ever written. Someday you will be able to read the Bible for yourself. God likes it when we read the Bible.

SOME QUESTIONS TO ANSWER
1. What is the name of God's very special book?
2. What does the Bible tell us about?
3. Can you think of any stories from the Bible?

A LITTLE PRAYER
Dear God, thank you for the Bible. Please help me do what it tells me to do.

A BIBLE VERSE FOR YOU TO LEARN
The whole Bible was given to us by inspiration from God.   2 TIMOTHY

3:16

Once I knew a little girl
Who liked to storm and pout.
If she's not careful, other kids
Will want to leave her out.

Do you see the little girl who is lying on the ground crying? I'm afraid she's making a big fuss about nothing. Do you ever do that? I hope not! God wants you to be happy. Here is what the little girl should do. She should stop crying and she should think about something nice. She could think about the nice friends God has given her, or she could think about her wonderful family. God has given her so much to be happy about. You talk to her now and tell her to be happy instead of mad. Say to her, "Little girl, please be happy because God loves you."

SOME QUESTIONS TO ANSWER
1. What are the children on the stage doing?
2. Why is the girl on the ground unhappy?
3. How can she be happy?

A LITTLE PRAYER
Dear Lord, help me to be happy all the time.

A BIBLE VERSE FOR YOU TO LEARN
Whatever happens, dear friends, be glad in the Lord. PHILIPPIANS 3:1

God made all the grass and birds,
The stars and moon and sun.
We worship him because he's God,
The great and mighty one.

At night when you look up into the sky, you can see the moon
and stars. In the day you can see the sun. God made all
these things, and he made the flowers and grass and you and
me. But some children don't know about God. They don't
know he made all these things, and they don't know God loves
them. Some children in other countries think there are many
gods, but there is really only one God. He made everything.
Missionaries go to tell people about God. Maybe someday
you can go and tell them too.

SOME QUESTIONS TO ANSWER
1. What do you see when you look into the sky at night?
2. Who made the moon and stars?
3. Is there more than one God?

A LITTLE PRAYER
Dear God, I know you are the only God there is. Thank you that
you love me.

A BIBLE VERSE FOR YOU TO LEARN
You may worship no other god than me. EXODUS 20:3

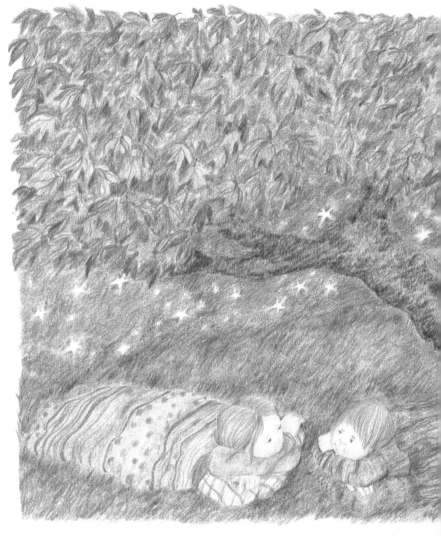

Idols made of wood or stone
Can't walk or talk or call.
We should not make or worship them,
For they're not God at all.

Do you know what an idol is? It is a piece of wood or stone carved to look like a bird or animal, or like a man or woman. You can see a picture of an idol in the book the mother is holding. The sad thing about idols is that some people in other countries think idols are alive! They bring gifts to the idols and pray to them! But God doesn't like this at all, because idols are not God and no one should ever pray to them. We must only worship the true God and never worship anything else. We need to go and tell the people who worship idols about the one true God.

SOME QUESTIONS TO ANSWER
1. Where is the idol in the picture?
2. Should people worship idols?
3. Whom should we worship?

A LITTLE PRAYER
Dear Father in heaven, help me always to worship only you.

A BIBLE VERSE FOR YOU TO LEARN
You shall not make any idols. EXODUS 20:4

God's name is very holy;
Do not use it as a curse.
Though dirty words should not be used,
To swear is even worse.

One of the boys in the picture is saying something very naughty, and the girl and the bears are holding their ears so they won't hear it. The boy is mad at his blocks and he said, "Oh, God!" but he wasn't thinking about God at all. That is wrong, and God says never to do it. His name is holy. It must be respected and honored, and not used carelessly. You can use God's name when you pray and when you are telling others about him, but not when you are just playing. Please remember this because it is so important to God.

SOME QUESTIONS TO ANSWER
1. What is happening in the picture?
2. Why are the bears holding their ears?
3. Should you say God's name or use naughty words when you are angry?

A LITTLE PRAYER
Dear Father in heaven, help me always to honor your holy name.

A BIBLE VERSE FOR YOU TO LEARN
You shall not use the name of Jehovah your God irreverently. EXODUS

20:7

Seven days are in each week,
But one's a special day.
And on that day we go to church
To worship and to pray.

The children's choir is singing songs of thanks and praise to God. When God created the world he gave us a special day of rest every week. He wants his people to stop their work and take time to think about him. He tells us to meet together with others of his people, and pray together and sing his praises and learn from the Bible and talk about God's love. Some people forget to do this, or else they don't care about what God wants. I hope you make God happy by going to church every week.

SOME QUESTIONS TO ANSWER

1. What are the children in the picture doing?
2. Can you name the seven days of the week?
3. Which one is a special day to rest and go to church?

A LITTLE PRAYER

Dear God, thank you that we can go to church to worship you.

A BIBLE VERSE FOR YOU TO LEARN

Remember to observe the Sabbath as a holy day. EXODUS 20:8

God says to obey your parents;
Do it with a smile.
So don't be grouchy, mad, or sad—
Try smiling for a while.

Look what a nice thing these children are doing! They have made breakfast for their father and mother and are serving it to them while they are still in bed. The children are honoring their parents. They are showing their love and respect. In the Bible God tells children to obey their fathers and mothers. That means doing what they tell you to do without getting grouchy or talking back. Your parents know what is best for you and what is dangerous or wrong. So you must obey and honor them. That makes God very happy.

SOME QUESTIONS TO ANSWER
1. What are the children doing?
2. Why are they doing it?
3. Should you talk back to your parents?

A LITTLE PRAYER
Dear God, help me to honor and obey my mother and father even when I don't feel like it.

A BIBLE VERSE FOR YOU TO LEARN
Honor your father and mother. EXODUS 20:12

Anger can be dangerous,
For it can make you bad.
So turn it off and then forgive,
And that will make God glad.

The children in the picture are throwing rocks and trying to hurt each other. The bears are hiding behind the trees. They know it is wrong for the children to do this. I'm sorry the children don't know this too. If you see someone in a movie or on TV hurting and killing people, say to yourself, "No, that is very wrong." God says we should not kill people. It is wrong to hate people too, even if they have hurt you or done something wrong to you. God says you should forgive them and love them.

SOME QUESTIONS TO ANSWER
1. Why are the bears hiding?
2. Does God want people to kill each other?
3. Is it OK to hate other people?

A LITTLE PRAYER
Dear Father in heaven, please help me not to hate other people, even if they're mean to me.

A BIBLE VERSE FOR YOU TO LEARN
You must not murder. EXODUS 20:13

A boy grows up, becomes a man,
And then he gets a wife.
The Bible says that they should stay
Together all their life.

Oh, look! It's a wedding! Everyone is happy and excited. Do you see the children's parents standing there watching? God gives mothers and fathers to one another to take care of each other and to take care of their children. God knows it is best for children to have both a mother and a father, so he tells parents always to keep on loving each other. Sometimes fathers or mothers don't obey God and don't love each other anymore, but that makes God unhappy. So if you get married, always love your husband or wife and not someone else instead.

SOME QUESTIONS TO ANSWER

1. Does God want mothers and fathers always to love each other?
2. How can you tell that the parents in the picture love each other?
3. If you get married when you grow up, will you always love your husband or wife?

A LITTLE PRAYER

Dear God, please help mothers and fathers everywhere to keep on loving each other.

A BIBLE VERSE FOR YOU TO LEARN

You must not commit adultery. EXODUS 20:14

When you're older you will find
That some kids like to steal.
They hide the gum and slip away—
How sad that makes God feel.

Oh, no! I see a girl stealing some candy. She is putting it in her purse instead of paying for it. The lady at the candy counter isn't looking. But someone is watching. God sees the girl doing this, and he is very sad. Did you ever take something that wasn't yours, and hide it? I hope not, for that is stealing. If you have stolen something, please give it back and tell the person you are sorry. Then tell God you are sorry. He will forgive you. God is glad when we obey him by not stealing.

SOME QUESTIONS TO ANSWER

1. What kind of store is in the picture?
2. What does stealing mean? Who in the picture is stealing?
3. Is it OK to steal things from a store?

A LITTLE PRAYER

Dear God, help me never to take things that don't belong to me.

A BIBLE VERSE FOR YOU TO LEARN

You must not steal. EXODUS 20:15

Tell the truth no matter what;
It's best at any time.
For telling lies just makes things
    worse;
It really is a crime.

Can you see that a cookie is missing from the cookie pan?
I wonder where it is? Oh, now I see it! Look what the boy is
holding behind his back! His big sister is asking him if he
took it, and I'm sorry to say he's telling a lie. He is saying he did
not take it. God is very unhappy when his children don't
tell the truth. Why is the boy afraid to tell the truth? I think it's
because he knows he will be scolded or punished. But he
should be brave and do what is right and say, "Yes, I took
it." I hope he doesn't lie again.

SOME QUESTIONS TO ANSWER
1. Where is the cookie?
2. What is a lie?
3. Does God want us to tell lies?

A LITTLE PRAYER
Dear Father in heaven, help me to remember always to tell
the truth.

A BIBLE VERSE FOR YOU TO LEARN
You must not lie. EXODUS 20:16

Thank the Lord for all you have;
Then if the neighbor boys
Get newer trucks or bigger trikes,
You'll still like your own toys.

Have you ever wished you had a toy that belongs to your friend? The Bible says it isn't good to want other people's things. God wants you to be happy with what you have, instead of being sad about things you don't have. In the picture you can see a little girl with a wagon who wants a Bigwheel instead. She is angry because her friend has a Bigwheel and she doesn't. But God doesn't always let you have everything you want. You should thank him for everything you have instead of being sorry you don't have more.

SOME QUESTIONS TO ANSWER

1. What does the girl in the picture wish she had?
2. Should you be sorry and mad if someone has a nicer toy than you have?
3. Are you thankful for all the nice things you have? What are some of them?

A LITTLE PRAYER

Dear God, thank you for giving me so many nice things.

A BIBLE VERSE FOR YOU TO LEARN

You must not be envious of your neighbor's house . . . or anything else

he has. EXODUS 20:17

WISE WORDS for little people

A WORD TO PARENTS (and Grandparents)

The Bible's proverbs contain great truths that even small children need to know. Some proverbs are easier than others to understand and apply to a child's world. I have carefully selected some of these and made them live for today. As with each of the other books in this series, my prayer is that very young lives will be directed toward godly living. This small book, containing God's Word, can have a life-changing effect. I hope you will pray that the Spirit of God will take the message of each page and plant it deep in your child's heart.

KENNETH N. TAYLOR

P.S. Don't forget to look for the ladybugs in every picture!

Here's a secret you should know
To make your friends feel glad.
Just tell them all how nice they are,
And then they can't be sad!

Has anyone ever told you how good you look, or said something else nice about you? If so, I think you liked hearing it. It makes us feel good when someone says something nice about us. We should remember to say nice things about others, too. In this picture the children are helping each other and saying, "You ski very well. You look great." They are making each other feel good. God doesn't want us to say bad things about people, but to make them happy instead. I hope you will be like the children in the picture.

SOME QUESTIONS TO ANSWER
1. Can you think of something nice to say about someone you know? (Maybe it will be your father or mother or your friend or brother or sister.)
2. Did it make you feel good to say something nice about that person?

A LITTLE PRAYER
Thank you, God, for my friends. Help me to encourage them by saying kind things about them.

A BIBLE VERSE FOR YOU TO LEARN
The Lord delights in kind words. PROVERBS 15:26

Shadow is a guinea pig
That likes to run and play.
Keri is in charge of it;
She feeds it every day.

How many pets can you see in the picture? Pets are a lot of fun, but they can't take care of themselves. Do you know that God wants us to take care of our pets? He doesn't want us to forget to feed them or to clean their cages or give them water. That would be mean and cruel. God is happy when we are kind to animals. He made them, and he wants us to take care of them for him. Are you a good "taker-carer" of your pets? I hope so.

SOME QUESTIONS TO ANSWER
1. Do you have a pet? What is its name?
2. Can you remember a time when you forgot to take care of your pet? Was it sad? What did it say?
3. Is God happy when you take care of your pet?

A LITTLE PRAYER
Dear God, thank you for making my pets. Help me to take good care of them.

A BIBLE VERSE FOR YOU TO LEARN
Good people are concerned for the welfare of their animals. PROVERBS

12:10

Jenny said, "Don't help me!"
As she started down the stairs.
But then they all went flying—
All her toys and little bears.

A little girl named Jenny thought she knew everything. She didn't want anybody to give her advice. She would say, "Don't help me, I'm big. I can do it all by myself." One day Jenny tried to take a wagon downstairs. Her mother had warned her not to do it, but she wouldn't listen. Now look what happened. I'm glad Jenny wasn't hurt, but she should have listened to her mother. God wants us to listen to what our friends and parents think is best for us. It is foolish not to listen to good advice.

SOME QUESTIONS TO ANSWER
1. What happened to Jenny?
2. Do you always want to do things your own way?
3. Does God want you to listen to what your friends and parents have to say?

A LITTLE PRAYER
Dear God, help me always to want your way and not just my own way.

A BIBLE VERSE FOR YOU TO LEARN
A fool thinks he needs no advice, but a wise man listens to others.

PROVERBS 12:15

The Bible is a special book.
It helps us to obey.
So read the Bible if you can,
A little every day.

In this picture, Lindsay and Stephen are listening to Bible stories. The other children are reading by themselves. They like to read stories from the Bible about Moses and King David and Esther. They expecially like the stories about Jesus and the wonderful things he did. Jesus made blind people see, and sick people well. Someday you will be able to read the Bible and read all of these things for yourself. That is something for you to look forward to.

SOME QUESTIONS TO ANSWER
1. What do we call God's special book?
2. Do you have a book of stories from the Bible? If not, ask your mother or father to get one for you.
3. Can you think of any stories from the Bible? Tell about one.

A LITTLE PRAYER
Dear God, thank you for the Bible. Help me to read it so I can know and do what you want me to.

A BIBLE VERSE FOR YOU TO LEARN
Despise God's Word and find yourself in trouble. Obey it and succeed.

PROVERBS 13:13

"Yes, I'll do it," said the boy,
"I'll do it right away."
But he forgot what he had said,
And he ran off to play.

Have I ever told you about a boy named Jamie? He had a "forgetter" in his head! He'd promise something and then forget about it. You could never believe him. His words didn't mean a thing. One day he promised to rake some leaves in the yard if his mother would let him play with his friends first. But she said, "No, I don't believe you. You have a hard time keeping your promises." So Jamie had to stay home to rake leaves. After that, Jamie learned to do what he promised. Now his mother believes him. She is happy, and he is happy, too. Remember always to keep your promises.

SOME QUESTIONS TO ANSWER
1. What did Jamie's mother want him to do?
2. Why wouldn't his mother let him play with his friends?
3. Can you think of something you said you would do but then didn't do?

A LITTLE PRAYER
Thank you, God, for always doing what you say. Help me always to keep my promises.

A BIBLE VERSE FOR YOU TO LEARN
God delights in those who keep their promises. PROVERBS 12:22

If you're acting naughty,
Your parents may spank you.
But when you get older,
You'll want to say, "Thank you!"

Oh my, what is happening to Little Bear? I think he was getting into the medicine cabinet. His mother told him not to, but he did it anyway. So now he is getting a spanking! Spankings and other kinds of punishment make you unhappy, but they also help you to be good. If your parents let you do bad things like lying and stealing and disobeying, you will probably grow up to be bad and unhappy. After you have been punished, your father and mother hug and kiss you. Then you feel good again, and you know that they love you. They want to keep you from being bad.

SOME QUESTIONS TO ANSWER
1. What did Little Bear do that was wrong?
2. Do you ever get punished? For what?
3. What are some ways your mother and father punish you?

A LITTLE PRAYER
Father in heaven, help me to obey and to be kind and good. Even though it hurts, thank you that I am punished when I disobey.

A BIBLE VERSE FOR YOU TO LEARN
Punishment that hurts chases evil from the heart. PROVERBS 20:30

Please have a little patience!
Don't push and kick and fight.
Sometimes you'll tire of waiting,
But you'll be doing right.

It isn't fun to wait and wait for your turn, but think what it would be like if everyone wanted to be first! There would be a lot of unhappiness and pushing and shoving and crying. In the picture you can see some children who are being patient and waiting for their turn. But I see two boys who aren't being patient at all. They are arguing over who should get the red car. If you were in the picture, what would you be doing? I hope you would be waiting patiently. God wants us to be patient and fair.

SOME QUESTIONS TO ANSWER
1. What are the children in the picture doing?
2. Which ones are arguing?
3. What should they do instead?

A LITTLE PRAYER
Dear Father in heaven, help me to learn to be patient and to wait for my turn.

A BIBLE VERSE FOR YOU TO LEARN
Be patient and you will finally win. PROVERBS 25:15

Don't say that someone did it When you know it isn't true. That's just as bad as hitting; It's a thing you shouldn't do.

Oh, what is happening in the picture? First, Emily broke a cup and is trying to hide the pieces under the table. Can you see them there? Now she's pointing at Heather and saying that Heather broke the cup. Is that good? No, it is not good at all! If you break something and then say somebody else broke it, you are telling a lie and being very unfair to the other person. So if you break something, you should say, "I'm sorry. I did it." Be brave and say so when you have been careless, or done something wrong. God wants us to be brave and honest and fair.

SOME QUESTIONS TO ANSWER
1. Can you see someone in the picture who is telling a lie? What is her name?
2. What should you say to God if you tell a lie? What should you say to the other person?

A LITTLE PRAYER
Dear God, I am sorry if I have told lies. Help me always to tell the truth. I want to make you happy by doing what is right.

A BIBLE VERSE FOR YOU TO LEARN
Telling lies about someone is as harmful as hitting him. PROVERBS 25:

See the children talk to God.
He likes it when we pray.
You can't see him, but he smiles
And hears you every day.

What is everyone doing in the picture? That's right, they are praying. They are talking to God. God is glad when you talk to him because he loves you. You talk to other people, so you should talk to God, too. He is right here in the room with you, even though you can't see him. What should you say to God? You can tell him you love him. You can thank him for all the good things he does for you. You can thank him for your parents and for your friends. You can tell him about your hurts. God is happy when you talk to him.

SOME QUESTIONS TO ANSWER
1. What are the children in the picture doing?
2. Does God like to hear you pray?
3. What are some things you can thank him for?

A LITTLE PRAYER
(say this silently in your heart without using your mouth)
Dear God, I love you. Help me to talk to you often.

A BIBLE VERSE FOR YOU TO LEARN
The Lord delights in the prayers of his people. PROVERBS 15:8

Be fair in everything you do;
Play fair in every game.
Don't mind at all
if you should lose—
Be happy just the same.

Can you see the games the children are playing? Most of them are having a happy time. But I see something I don't like! In the center of the picture Jason is leaning over and peeking at someone else's cards! He's not playing fair. He's not playing by the rules. He is cheating. He wants to win more than he wants to do what is right. But God wants us to be fair, even if it means we will lose. If we win we must win fairly. So if you want to make God happy, don't cheat.

SOME QUESTIONS TO ANSWER
1. Point to Jason. What is he doing? Is he being fair?
2. Can you think of a time when you weren't being fair? Tell about it.
3. How can you make God happy when you play?

A LITTLE PRAYER
Dear Lord, please help me always to be fair and not to cheat.

A BIBLE VERSE FOR YOU TO LEARN
The Lord demands fairness. PROVERBS 16:11

Be careful, my children;
Don't go with a stranger.
His words may sound good,
But he might bring you danger.

Your parents have probably told you not to get into a car with a person you don't know. Do you know why? Because sometimes strangers who seem nice aren't nice at all. A stranger might say, "I will give you some candy if you ride with me in my car." Or he might say that he will show you his puppies or kittens. But don't do it. He might be a bad person who would hurt you if you went with him. The best thing to do is to run away from him. Don't stay and talk to him. The girl in the picture is running away from the man who offered her a lollipop. She is doing the right thing.

SOME QUESTIONS TO ANSWER
1. What is the girl in the picture doing?
2. What should you do if a stranger wants you to ride or walk with him?
3. What would you do if he said he would give you some candy? What if he wanted to show you his puppies or kittens?

A LITTLE PRAYER
Dear God, help me to listen to my parents and not to someone I don't know.

A BIBLE VERSE FOR YOU TO LEARN
Pretty words may hide a wicked heart. PROVERBS 26:23

Always be honest;
Don't cheat or lie.
Be truthful with others
And don't make them cry.

Justin was playing in the yard and found some money. He thought, *This is mine because I found it, and now I can buy some candy.* Just then Kristen came out of the house carrying her purple purse. She was crying. "I've lost my money. Have you seen it anywhere?" Justin thought about the yummy candy. "No, I haven't seen your money," he lied. Later Justin thought, *I shouldn't have said that.* He went into the house and said to Kristen, "I'm sorry," and then gave her the money he had found. She was glad because she had her money again, and God was glad because Justin had finally told the truth.

SOME QUESTIONS TO ANSWER
1. What did Justin find while he was playing?
2. What did he do with the money he found?
3. Can you think of a time you were honest even though it was hard?

A LITTLE PRAYER
Dear God, help me always to be honest.

A BIBLE VERSE FOR YOU TO LEARN
The Lord hates cheating and delights in honesty. PROVERBS 11:1

Can you do some things better
Than any other kid?
Remember, God is helping you,
So don't be acting big!

In the picture, Sarah is acting like she thinks she is better than all the other children. She thinks she is the best one in the class. Sometimes she even says, "I'm better than you are!" She is being selfish and proud. This is not good. Do you ever act like Sarah? If you do, please don't do it anymore. If you are especially good at coloring or tumbling or playing a game, remember it is because God is helping you. So don't be proud about it. That would make God sad. Say "Thank you" to God instead of thinking you're so great.

SOME QUESTIONS TO ANSWER
1. What is Sarah doing?
2. Can you do some things better than the other children can?
3. Should you be proud about it? Why not?

A LITTLE PRAYER
Father in heaven, thank you for the things I am good at doing. Thank you for helping me.

A BIBLE VERSE FOR YOU TO LEARN
Pride goes before a fall! PROVERBS 16:18

Who took care of Daddy
When he was just a lad?
Your grandma did, and grandpa too,
So show them you are glad.

In this picture you can see the children talking to their grandmother and grandfather. They are having a happy time. God wants you to make your grandparents happy because they took good care of your mother or father many years ago. You should say "Thank you" to your grandparents for all they have done. One good way of thanking them is to make them happy. You could write a letter or talk to them on the telephone. Maybe you can visit them or invite them to come and visit you. That will make them happy, and God will be happy too.

SOME QUESTIONS TO ANSWER
1. What do you call your grandparents?
2. How can you make your grandparents happy?
3. Why should we try to make our grandparents happy?

A LITTLE PRAYER
Dear God, thank you for my grandparents. Help me to make them happy.

A BIBLE VERSE FOR YOU TO LEARN
An old man's grandchildren are his crowning glory. PROVERBS 17:6

Getting mad is foolish.
It doesn't help a bit!
Instead, control your temper—
Don't kick or bite or hit!

In the picture you can see a boy named Adam. He was playing a table game with his sister, Meg. He didn't win, so he knocked the game off the table and is running into the other room. Now he won't play anymore. I think he is being a poor sport, don't you? He got mad about losing. But God doesn't want people to act that way. He wants us to learn to be happy even when we lose. In the other part of the picture you can see Adam being sorry about what he did. Now he is pushing Meg on the swing instead of being angry. Adam is learning to control his temper.

SOME QUESTIONS TO ANSWER
1. Why did Adam run away from his sister?
2. Was he being a good sport?
3. Does God want us to be happy even when we lose?

A LITTLE PRAYER
Father in heaven, please help me to be happy even when I lose.

A BIBLE VERSE FOR YOU TO LEARN
A wise man restrains his anger. PROVERBS 19:11

If you wake up really early
And your parents are asleep,
Be quiet as a little mouse—
And don't let out a peep!

Everyone in the picture is asleep except Kimberley. She woke up a long time before breakfast and before anyone else. Now she is quietly reading a book. She is as quiet as a little mouse because she knows the other people in the house want to sleep. She isn't playing with her drum or listening to the radio because she knows the loud sounds would wake everyone up. The next time you wake up early, pretend you are a little mouse! See how quiet you can be!

SOME QUESTIONS TO ANSWER
1. Do your parents like loud noise early in the morning?
2. What can you play with if you wake up early?
3. What little animal should you try to be like if you wake up early?

A LITTLE PRAYER
Dear God, thank you that I can rest when I am tired. But help me to be quiet when I wake up before anyone else.

A BIBLE VERSE FOR YOU TO LEARN
If you shout a pleasant greeting to a friend too early in the morning,

he will count it as a curse! PROVERBS 27:14

Don't be mad
when Mother scolds you;
Please don't fuss and pout.
It only means she wants to help,
Of that there is no doubt.

Why is Mother Bear unhappy with Little Bear? It is because Little Bear knocked all the oranges off the table. Can you see them on the floor? Mother Bear is telling Little Bear not to do it again. But I see something I don't like. Little Bear is pouting and sulking instead of saying, "I'm sorry, I won't do it again." If you do something wrong, admit it! Don't feel sorry for yourself if your mother needs to scold you. Be glad that she wants you to do what is right.

SOME QUESTIONS TO ANSWER
1. Why is Little Bear's mother scolding him?
2. Tell about a time you were scolded. Did you pout or become angry? What should you do instead?

A LITTLE PRAYER
Father in heaven, thank you for people who love me, who tell me to stop doing things that are wrong.

A BIBLE VERSE FOR YOU TO LEARN
It is a badge of honor to accept valid criticism. PROVERBS 25:12

Stephanie's having a party—
See all the children play.
For days and days she's
planned and planned;
What fun she'll have today!

What is happening in the picture? The children are having a party! What are the little bears doing? Everyone will have a good time. Whom do you think Stephanie invited to her party? I think she invited her friends. But she also invited some other children who just moved into the house down the street. She doesn't know them very well, but she wanted them to come, too. That was a nice thing for Stephanie to do. God likes us to be kind. He is happy with us when we do nice things for other people to make them happy.

SOME QUESTIONS TO ANSWER
1. Is there someone you don't know very well whom you could invite to a party? Who?
2. Think of a way besides having a party to make someone happy.

A LITTLE PRAYER
Dear God, thank you that I can do things to make other people happy.

A BIBLE VERSE FOR YOU TO LEARN
Joy fills hearts that are planning for good. PROVERBS 12:20

Taffy was a little bear
Who had a friend named Tad.
But once she said that Tad looked dumb,
And that made him feel sad.

Can you guess what the children and bears are doing?
They're getting ready for a play. It looks like everyone is
having a good time. But two of the bears are unhappy.
Taffy is pointing at Tad and said he looks dumb. Of course,
that hurt Tad's feelings. I think we should tell Taffy something important. Let's tell her, "Taffy, don't say things that
hurt other people's feelings. God wants us to be kind to
each other and to love each other." I hope Taffy tells Tad
she's sorry. Then Tad will feel better, and they will be
friends again.

SOME QUESTIONS TO ANSWER
1. What are the children and bears doing?
2. Should Taffy say unkind things to her friend?
3. Can God help Taffy tell Tad she's sorry? Can he help you
   when you are unhappy with someone?

A LITTLE PRAYER
Dear God, please help me to be kind to everyone, and to
like them.

A BIBLE VERSE FOR YOU TO LEARN
Some people like to make cutting remarks, but the words of the wise

soothe and heal. PROVERBS 12:18

Good is good and bad is bad,
And never the twain shall meet.
So do not say that bad is good,
Or that stealing can be neat.

Look what's happening in this picture! Joshua and Matt are taking Jeremy's bike while he isn't looking. That's not right. That's stealing! But that's not all. They're telling their friend Carlos that it's okay to steal. "It's fun to take things from other people. And besides, Jeremy can get another bike." But stealing makes God sad. And it makes God angry when someone tries to get others to be bad. I hope Carlos will be brave enough to tell his friends not to take the bike.

SOME QUESTIONS TO ANSWER
1. What are Joshua and Matt going to steal?
2. Jeremy isn't watching them, but Someone sees what they are doing. Do you know who it is?
3. Should you do what is wrong if your friends say it is okay?

A LITTLE PRAYER
Dear God, help me to say "No" when someone wants me to do something bad.

A BIBLE VERSE FOR YOU TO LEARN
The Lord despises those who say that bad is good, and good is bad.

PROVERBS 17:15

Rebecca is a little girl
Who puts her toys away.
When Mother says, "Please do it now,"
Rebecca will obey.

This little girl's name is Rebecca. She is a happy little girl, but sometimes she doesn't like to put away her toys when it is time to go to bed! One day when a baby-sitter was taking care of her, she thought, *Tonight I won't need to put away my toys because my parents aren't home.* But then she thought, *I should do what my parents want me to,* even *though they aren't here.* So she is putting her toys away. Her parents will be happy when they come home and find everything put away. God is happy, too, because Rebecca is obeying her father and mother.

SOME QUESTIONS TO ANSWER
1. What is Rebecca doing?
2. What is something you can do to make your father and mother happy?
3. Does it make your parents happy when you obey them?

A LITTLE PRAYER
Dear God, help me to want to do whatever my parents tell me to.

A BIBLE VERSE FOR YOU TO LEARN
Give your parents joy. PROVERBS 23:25

Give thanks to God
For a father's love
And for his prayers
To heaven above.

In the picture you can see a father getting books from the library and reading to his children. You can see that the children like it when he reads to them. They know their father loves them, because he helps them and takes care of them. And I'll tell you a secret. Every day their father prays for them. God listens to his prayers and helps the children in many ways. He sends his angels to be with them, and he helps the children to be kind and good. Your father prays for you, and you should pray for him. Thank God every day for giving your father to you.

SOME QUESTIONS TO ANSWER
1. Maybe the father in the picture is reading one of the books you like. Which of your books do you think it might be?
2. When could you pray for your father and mother and brother or sister?

A LITTLE PRAYER
Dear Father in heaven, thank you for giving me a mother and father. Please help them to make me a good person, and help them to love you.

A BIBLE VERSE FOR YOU TO LEARN
A child's glory is his father. PROVERBS 17:6

Some boys and girls have many clothes,
And some don't have enough.
But we're not better if we own
A lot of toys and stuff.

Pretty clothes are nice, but not everybody has them. Some boys and girls come from families that don't have very much money. Their parents can't buy them new clothes and toys. Sometimes children who have lots of nice things act as if they are better than the children who don't have very much. But that is being foolish and unkind. If God gives you a lot of nice things, don't be proud about it. Instead, be thankful to God for giving you so much. And if your family does not have much money, you still have many things to be thankful for. And remember that God loves you just as much as he loves anyone.

SOME QUESTIONS TO ANSWER
1. Do you see the children in the picture whose clothes are not so pretty?
2. Does God love children more if they have lots of clothes and toys?
3. Does God love children just as much if they don't have lots of clothes and toys?

A LITTLE PRAYER
Father in heaven, thank you for all you have given me. Help me to like everyone I know, whether they are rich or poor.

A BIBLE VERSE FOR YOU TO LEARN
To despise the poor is to sin. Blessed are those who pity them.

PROVERBS 14:21

If you know what's right,
Don't do what is wrong,
No matter who says,
"It's okay, come along!"

Oh, Katie, don't do that! Can you see what she is doing? She is stealing a cookie. Her brother took one and said it was okay. Their mother said not to, but Katie is disobeying anyway. Katie is doing wrong just because her brother did! That is not good at all. When you know something is wrong, don't do it, even if someone else tells you it's okay. God is happy when you obey your parents and do what is right. He is unhappy when you listen to what you know is wrong.

SOME QUESTIONS TO ANSWER
1. Where are Katie and her family?
2. What is Katie doing with the cookie?
3. Should you ever say it's okay to do something you know is wrong?

A LITTLE PRAYER
Dear God, please help me always to do what I know is right and not listen to anyone who tries to get me to do something wrong.

A BIBLE VERSE FOR YOU TO LEARN
Stop listening to teaching that contradicts what you know is right.

PROVERBS 19:27

Little bears, stop fighting!
Will you never learn?
Please don't be so selfish—
Let others have a turn.

Oh, dear me! Look at the little bears. They are pushing and quarreling. They aren't being nice to each other at all. They both want to ride on the rocking horse. But neither of them can play with it while they are fighting. What should they do instead? That's right. They can take turns or even ride the horse together. They are being silly because they aren't sharing. Have you ever been foolish by fighting instead of sharing? I hope not, but if you have been, please don't be foolish anymore. Everyone should have a turn.

SOME QUESTIONS TO ANSWER
1. What are the bears fighting about?
2. What should they do instead of fighting?
3. Tell about a time you shared a toy with someone.

A LITTLE PRAYER
Father in heaven, please help me to share and not quarrel.

A BIBLE VERSE FOR YOU TO LEARN
It is an honor to stay out of a fight. Only fools insist on quarreling.

PROVERBS 20:3

Shut your eyes and hold them closed—
Now try to walk around.
Thank God for eyes that look and see
And ears that hear the sound.

In the picture you can see a little bear helping a lady cross the street. The lady can't see anything because she is blind. Shut your eyes and walk around, and you'll feel what it is like to be blind. Blind people live all their lives in darkness. But it is amazing how well they can walk around. Some use a white cane to help them feel if a table or chair is in their way, and some have a specially trained dog to guide them when they are outside. How thankful to God we should be because we can see and hear.

SOME QUESTIONS TO ANSWER
1. Can you point to the woman in the picture who is blind?
2. Why does she have a white cane?
3. Do you know anyone who is blind or who can't hear well?

A LITTLE PRAYER
Thank you so much, dear God, for eyes that see and ears that hear. Please help me to help anyone who can't see or hear as well as I do.

A BIBLE VERSE FOR YOU TO LEARN
If you have good eyesight and good hearing, thank God who gave them

to you. PROVERBS 20:12

ABOUT THE AUTHOR

Kenneth N. Taylor is best known as the translator of *The Living Bible*, but his first renown was as a writer of children's books. Ken and his wife, Margaret, have ten children, and his early books were written for use in the family's daily devotions. The manuscripts were ready for publication only when they passed the scrutiny of those ten young critics! Those books, which have now been read to two generations of children around the world, include *The Bible in Pictures for Little Eyes* (Moody Press), *Stories for the Children's Hour* (Moody Press), and *The Living Bible Story Book* (Tyndale House). Now the Taylor children are all grown, so *Wise Words for Little People, Big Thoughts for Little People*, and *Giant Steps for Little People* were written with the numerous grandchildren in mind.

Ken Taylor is a graduate of Wheaton College and Northern Baptist Seminary. He is the founder and chairman of Tyndale House Publishers. He and Margaret live in Wheaton, Illinois.

ABOUT THE ILLUSTRATOR

Kathryn E. Shoemaker has had broad experience as an art teacher, curriculum specialist, filmmaker, and illustrator. Her published works include twenty books, eight filmstrips, illustrations for many magazine articles, and numerous educational in-service materials. She is a strong advocate of the involvement of parents in the local schools, and spends a great deal of time as a volunteer in her children's school. She is also a volunteer with the Canadian Mental Health Association and the Red Cross.

Kathryn is a graduate of Immaculate Heart College in Los Angeles. She also studied at Chouinards Art Institute, Otis Art Institute, and Occidental College, and is a member of the Society of Illustrators. She and her two children, Kristen and Andrew, who helped critique the illustrations for the *Little People* books, live in Vancouver, British Columbia.